Transactional Analysis on the Job

By Charles Albano

amacom
A division of American Management Associations

Reprinted from *Supervisory Management*

International standard book number: 0-8144-6940-x

Fifth printing

Foreword

Transactional Analysis on the Job is intended to fill a need for systematic treatment of selected transactional analysis concepts having immmediate applicability to supervisor-employee relations. As I see it, today's supervisor tends to be exposed in a hit-or-miss way to a wealth of psychological concepts of varying degrees of utility and suggesting very different practices. Sometimes these are contradictory; even more often, they address only a corner of human reality and not the whole person. The upshot of this is that the supervisor finds himself without a complete or self-consistent framework for dealing with the human problems that are peculiar to employee relations. When this happens, the supervisor is forced to relate pieces of theory in tinker-toy fashion to problems demanding immediate resolution. This can lead to uneven success at best, and abandonment of useful approaches at worst.

It seems to me that one vital contribution of TA lies in its power to deal with the entire range of human behavior in a consistent and understandable way. With TA we have a "whole person" approach to understanding self and others that fosters appropriate emphasis on how we relate to one another. This kind of emphasis on interpersonal relations lies at the heart of supervision and suggests, quite correctly, that the things that go on between us can be modified to mutual advantage if we are sensitive to them.

The core issues in supervisor-employee relations have to do with mutual trust and respect. These are conveyed through our communications and our behavior. They are the outgrowth of genuine concern for individuals. Effective supervisors know that no set of techniques can ever replace integrity and sincerity in our relationships. Overemphasis on "handling" people may lead us to overlook our need to communicate about our very habits of communication. Sometimes we treat these habits as though they were unalterable. But TA can help us to change our patterns of interaction in a rational and appropriate manner.

It is the untested assumptions that we make about each other that keep us apart and plague our communications. If there is one lesson to be learned about human relations it is this: Understanding another person is a process in motion and not a finished product. There is danger in having a fixed evaluation of others that is not open to change with new experience. TA can provide a means to view each contact with others as a fresh and unique occurrence; yet it encourages us to be sensitive to meaningful patterns. In our search for understanding we must shun the habits of being label-prone or of supervising as though we were calculating machines. The ultimate aim of TA is to let us be ourselves, effectively. If this book helps promote interpersonal understanding and group effectiveness at work, it will have fulfilled its purpose.

Charles Albano

Although Mr. Albano is an employment development specialist, Army Electronics Command, Fort Monmouth, N.J. the views expressed in these articles do not necessarily represent official thinking or endorsement by any agency of the Department of the Army.

Contents

part 1:
How we're programmed

Boss: "Helen, can I have the contract file for this quarter?"

Helen: "Do you want the file with the blue tab or the file with the yellow tab?"

Boss (sighing resignedly): "You know the one I need, Helen. Just give me the current file."

Helen: "Is that the one that contains the Adams letter?"

Boss (raising his eyebrows): "Well, that's a current contract item, isn't it?"

Helen: "Oh, I think I misfiled it."

Boss (completely exasperated): "Forget it! I'll find it myself. You can't do anything right, can you?"

This dialogue illustrates the game that transactional analysts call STUPID. Helen, who is not a new employee, initiates the game in the role of Victim. And she wins the game: She gets from her boss what she was angling for—a putdown. Another game Helen likes to play is KICK ME. The drift of this game is like that of STUPID, but the payoff is much harsher. She invariably manipulates her bosses (of which she has had quite a few) into the role of Persecutor.

This and other kinds of games (which we'll discuss more fully later on) certainly aren't in the interest of efficiency or any other company goal. What's more, they're a drain on the emotional energy of the people locked into them. So why do people play such self-defeating games?

Many psychologists and laymen alike see promising answers to this question in transactional analysis (TA), an approach to analyzing human behavior—in particular, the "transactions" that people make when they communicate with each other. TA was originated by Dr. Eric Berne, a clinical psychiatrist whose best-selling book, *Games People Play,* did a lot to popularize TA and generate widespread interest in his other books. The literature in the field is large and growing (see the list of references on page 10).

This article is the first in a series designed to:

1. Get across TA concepts that have management applications.

2. Illustrate these concepts by presenting and analyzing on-the-job transactions.

3. Link TA concepts to other behavioral concepts with which managers may already be familiar.

The concepts of TA and the language used to express them are simple. But they offer an impressive payoff: a way of understanding and exerting some control over your on-the-job behavior and that of others. With the insight provided by TA, you can, for example, avoid getting "hooked" into playing someone else's unproductive game. In fact, you may be able to stop the game and turn it into a straightforward transaction. You can also draw upon TA techniques to figure out:

- What prompts one subordinate to put another down "without cause."
- Why a fellow supervisor seems to behave naturally one moment and childishly the next.
- Why and how employees store up emotions that sap their vitality at work.
- Why your boss mistakenly takes offense at innocent remarks.
- Why, after talking to your boss's boss, you feel as though you've been talking to the top of an iceberg.
- Why you can't always find a rational explanation for an employee's behavior.

- Why some very talented people seem to go out of their way to display self-defeating behavior.
- Why some employees overreact to incidents of little significance.
- Why you find it difficult to think "straight" under stress.
- Why you are easily offended by some bosses and attracted to others.
- Why your thoughts are sometimes so different from your feelings.
- Why some people can't or won't accept sound advice.
- Why the same activity that appeals to some workers repels others.
- Why some employees repeatedly do things that bring the ceiling down on them.
- Why it is that one part of you says "go" on a project and another says "no."

Stroking

Basic to an understanding of the "transactions" people make when they communicate is the principle of stroking. In playing the game of STUPID described at the beginning of this article, Helen was looking for and got what transactional analysts call a *discount*—which is a negative form of stroking. Stroking is something we all must have, whether it's negative or positive. As infants and children, most of us *literally* received positive strokes—hugs, caresses, kisses—that made us feel good. Sometimes, however, we received negative strokes in the form of physical punishment or scoldings—and bad as they made us feel, they were preferable to no strokes at all. Studies have revealed, in fact, that children who receive only negative strokes or discounts will fare infinitely better than those who receive no strokes at all. It is even possible for infants to die in the total absence of stroking.

In later life, we continue to seek "stroking" in such forms of recognition as a greeting, a compliment on appearance, praise for performance. However, we may go after discounts if no other form of stroking is available or if we have become confirmed discount-seekers.

Everyone has experienced the pain or discomfort of discounts. A manager is discounted when his boss makes a habit of going around him to communicate directly with employees. You may experience a discount when you are neither consulted about nor invited to attend a meeting on matters for which you are responsible. You are discounted when impractical goals are established without your participation and then foisted upon you for implementation. You are discounted when you are not given courtesy copies of correspondence that you feel you should have. There are many, many ways of giving people discounts, and most can easily be avoided.

"The "climate" of a department or organization can be assessed by determining the stroking behavior of those in key positions and then correlating it with morale at working levels. Stroking patterns have a great deal to do with how we feel about going to work and about working once we get there.

A word of praise from a valued person at a "teachable moment" can spur an employee on to long-lasting efforts. Similarly, a single sharp discount at such a time can make it difficult for him to learn and perform well. Consider the effect of the following supervisor-to-employee discounts:

"You're not half the engineer that Ralph is."

"I'm not interested in your opinions."

"When I was your age, I had twice your experience."

The kinds of strokes we give and the kinds we seek have a telling impact on the kinds of transactions we make, the kinds of games we play. Before getting into these and other aspects of transactional analysis, however, let's take a look at the ego states that make it possible to analyze behavior.

Ego states

According to transactional analysts, every personality has three sets of programming, or ego states: Parent, Adult, and Child. (They are capital-

EGO-STATE CONTRIBUTIONS TO BEHAVIOR

What the Parent does	What the Adult does	What the Child does
Nurtures	Processes information	Invents
Criticizes	Takes objective action	Expresses curiosity
Restricts	Thinks, then acts	Acts on impulse
Judges	Organizes	Acts selfishly
Blames	Plans	Loves
Encourages	Solves problems	Imagines/brainstorms
Supports	Estimates risks	Acts belligerently
	Ferrets out assumptions	Complains
Source—the relationship between you and your parents.	*Source*—the emergence of independent thinking in early life and its subsequent development.	*Source*—the best and worst of your young self.

ized to differentiate them from their literal counterparts.) Individual behavior during transactions with another person is determined by the particular ego state in action at the time; the one that's activated depends on many factors—including early life experiences, the circumstances of the transaction, and the other person's ego state.

A person's behavior may stem most frequently from the same ego state—which is why we are often able to see typical or recurrent patterns of behavior. In a well-adjusted person, however, all three ego states function, with none substantially eclipsed by another. When we use them in a way appropriate to the reality of a situation, we are functioning most successfully.

Where do these ego states come from? How can we recognize them—in ourselves and in others? Let's start with the Parent ego state.

The Parent ego state

The Parent is the part of the personality containing all the instructions and guidance—the *should's, ought's, do's* and *dont's*—that we acquired through intimate association with our parents and other authority figures in our youth. The Parent ego state (like the other two) results from a learning process. In a vast mental file cabinet of recordings, we have stored an assortment of Parent rules for living; we draw upon and use them as occasions require.

From the TA standpoint, the personality is pretty well established by the time we are six to eight years old. This early schooling came from observing our parents relate to each other and interact with others. We listened, we watched, we drew lessons. The experience was both impressive and lasting. Our feelings, too, were "recorded" and filed away. It may be difficult to reconstruct a precise impression today of any of the myriad past events in our lives. We may not even be conscious of the existence of a great number of these recordings. But psychologists and, more recently, medical researchers assure us that these recordings are "live." They do influence the way we behave today.

The Parent ego state has two sides. Various transactional analysts have referred to them as the Nurturing Parent on the one hand, and the Critical or Prejudicial Parent on the other, to reflect the opposite ways in which parents behave toward children. That is, most parents not only shelter and help their children meet the physical and emotional needs of development (nurturing behavior)—they also punish their children, if only by restricting their activities (critical behavior).

As adults, therefore, we harbor both Nurturing Parent and Critical Parent impressions. We generally draw upon them in raising a family and,

significantly, in supervising subordinates. The influence of these recordings or tapes is reflected when we "come on Parent" in our dealings with
others. Whether a particular response is beneficial or detrimental depends
on how well suited it is to the occasion. Behavior copied and transposed
intact from our parents to a current situation can arouse hostility. Our
Critical Parent, for example, may unexpectedly assault a subordinate's
Child ego state. When we impulsively allow the Parent to assert itself

INDICATORS OF EGO STATES

	BODY LANGUAGE	EXPRESSIONS	VOCAL TONE
PARENT INDICATORS	Looking down over rim of glasses. Point-ing an accusing fin-ger. Hands on hip, the head leaning or straining forward. Patting on the back.	"You should . . . you ought . . . you must" "Why don't you . . ." "Stay loose" "Be cool" "Don't tell me . . ." "You disappoint me" "You always" "Poor thing" "I'll protect you"	Harsh Judgmental Soothing Indignant Commanding Comforting
ADULT INDICATORS	A straight, relaxed stance. Slightly tilted head. Appearance of active listening. Reg-ular eye contact. Confident ap-pearance.	The offer of alter-natives and options. Use of the 5 W's in questioning. "Aha, I see" "I see your point" "I recognize . . ." "How do you feel about . . ."	Relaxed Assertive Somewhat de-liberative Self-assertive
CHILD INDICATORS	Forlorn appearance. Drooping shoulders. Withdrawal. Pursed lips. Scowling. Skip-ping. Hugging. Twin-kle in eyes.	"I want" "I wish" "Wow" "I should" "If only" "Did I do okay?" "One of these days" "It's not fair" "It's not my fault" "Oh boy!"	Appealing Complaining Nagging Indignant Cheerful Protesting Grumbling Mumbling Sullen

before estimating the consequences, we may well regret having done so later on.

Once we know the nature and sources of our behavior, we can more easily adopt appropriate behavior and avoid inappropriate behavior. We can't change our pasts, but it certainly helps to take the past into account. The behavior we were taught may have become outdated or inappropriate for some other reason. Recent and current social changes mandate a careful look at Parent tapes. Consider, for example, how much prevailing views have changed concerning the value of work, the role of women, the rights of management, the responsibility of employees, and many other basic values. We must be sensitive to these changes and keep an open mind toward them and their implications. Knowing our Parent will help in this and will facilitate our ability to make necessary adjustments.

On the other hand, much Parent programming is valuable. Useful habits mastered under parental guidance can carry you when the going gets rough. Habits and automatic responses based on Parent tapes can streamline efforts to make minor decisions that might otherwise consume time and effort better spent on the things that count. Consulting the Parent before making an important decision can yield worthwhile guidance; in any event, being aware of its feelings about a particular matter is important whether the advice is taken or not. Why? Because this awareness reduces internal conflict between your Parent and your Child ego states. With awareness, you conserve energy that might be wasted on an undefined, unresolved conflict—a conflict that might, in fact, keep you from making a decision.

The Adult ego state

The Adult is the problem solver. Rational and objective, it provides clear thinking and analysis—fundamental skills in managing people and situations. A manager calls upon his Adult to stand apart for an objective consideration of Parent and Child feelings, attitudes, possible prejudices. It can help gather facts, separate them from opinion and inference, analyze them, compute the effects of alternatives, and select the best one. You can make your Adult more effective by continually examining your experiences and drawing lessons from them. Training courses in personnel management and human relations confront the manager in ways that cause him to do just that.

The Child ego state

Transactional analysts consider the Child ego state to be the most creative part of a personality. Behavior activated by the Child should be referred to as childlike, not childish. Childishness denotes immaturity —not the case in much Child-originated behavior. Like the Parent, however, the Child does initiate less desirable behavior.

The Child ego state has three parts: the Natural Child, the Manipulator, and the Adapted Child. The Natural Child is distinguished by its enjoyment of life, its need for affection, and its curiosity. The intense curiosity that the infant expresses by touching, pushing, and gripping everything in its range shows up later in laboratories, machine shops, and advertising agencies. When we don't lose too much curiosity in the process of

---

Your Adult Can Help You on the Job

Eric Berne has commented that the Adult performs executive functions. Before it can do so efficiently, however, it must moderate the confusion that results from conflict between Parent and Child—confusion that can keep us from attaining objectives in our best interest.

The following examples show the reaction of each ego state when the person involved is confronted with an on-the-job dilemma:

Joan is being considered for promotion to a supervisory position:

 "Women shouldn't be put in positions supervising men."

 "I can do this job and earn their allegiance. I accept the challenge."

 "These men won't like me if I'm promoted—but I want the job!"

Joan's Adult is well informed. It allows her the freedom she needs in order to be decisive.

George wants to delegate some of his workload—a difficult management function for many supervisors:

 "People are lazy. You can't turn your back on them."

 "Sam is competent. I've coached him and given him authority to act in my name."

 "If he fouls this up, I'm in trouble."

George's Adult recognized a subordinate's competence and set up conditions favorable to effective performance. A good delegator has a confident and skillful Adult.

growing up, it can spark outstanding performance, achievement, and discovery.

Our Natural Child also lets us act freely and openly with others. Transactions during this state can create feelings of warmth, friendliness, and acceptance—feelings that will satisfy our continuing need for affection. Playful, joking activity stems from the Natural Child. Creative people often describe creativity as a playful process, a toying with ideas, an urge to tinker with things and see what comes of it. Like humor, an exciting creation can result from putting things together that logically "don't belong together."

The Manipulator in the Child uses its potent, intuitive understanding of people to get its own sweet way. It is astute at gauging the limits of other people's endurance or tolerance. A master strategist, it can trick or con people into doing what it wants them to. We will examine its bargaining and game-playing prowess later. The Manipulator doesn't sound very constructive so far, but it can be. In toying intuitively with ideas and relationships, it can trigger inspiration, creation, and insight.

The Adapted Child results from the changes in our social behavior that we made as we grew up in order to be accepted by those around us. The roots of such behavior lie in past modes of conformity, obedience to authority, and the need to please others. A certain degree of conformity and adjustment is fine—but an overly adapted Child may hold us back today by keeping us from having full confidence in ourselves. When this happens, we fail to step out boldly in pursuit of our own inner needs and wants. An employee or a supervisor with an overadapted Child is afraid to try his wings and may fail unless he receives a lot of assurance from

References and Recommended Reading on Transactional Analysis

The author expresses his indebtedness to the following authors and sources:

Eric Berne:
Transactional Analysis in Psychotherapy, Grove Press, N.Y., 1961.
Games People Play, Grove Press, N.Y., 1964.
What Do You Say After You Say Hello? Grove Press, N.Y., 1972.

Thomas Harris:
I'm OK—You're OK, Harper, N.Y., 1969.

Muriel James and Dorothy Jongeward:
Born to Win: TA with Gestalt Experiments, Addison-Wesley, Mass., 1971.

those around him. He needs encouragement to take more initiative and he needs reassurance that failure is a legitimate part of learning. A very dependent person may literally have to be given permission to do his own thinking.

Ways to pinpoint ego states

You can pinpoint ego states if you know what to look for. Analyze posture, facial expression, and tone of voice as well as behavior—all four are important clues to the particular ego state in action. See page 12 for a categorization of such clues by ego state.

Although it is sometimes impossible to be absolutely sure in labelling an ego state, in many cases the origins of remarks are fairly clear. Consider the following remarks made in a shop during an on-the-job training program:

"Don't weaken. I know you can succeed with a little more effort." (Nurturing Parent)

"Do I really have to take your hand and walk you through this simple procedure?" (Critical Parent)

"I'll never get the hang of this." (Child)

"If I learn the theory, the practice will be easy." (Adult)

Contaminated thinking

Sometimes Parent opinions, attitudes, and thoughts appear to us to be genuine expressions of our own objective thinking. We may express them automatically and comfortably. But when someone challenges them, we really can't defend them properly; we realize that we have never given them much thought. This is the result when the Parent contaminates the Adult.

When we express Parent prejudices and opinions directly to others or base our actions on them, we may think we are acting objectively—but we are only transmitting playbacks of old recordings. Here are some remarks that reflect Parent contamination of the Adult:

"There's no way to be an individual in a large company."

"You can't depend on any woman in a position calling for cool judgment."

"The unions will drive this country to ruin."

The more the Adult can shut out automatic hand-downs from the Parent, the more independent and objective it can be.

The Child can also influence our Adult's thinking and actions by dredging up feelings tied to some past event. Child feelings can even eclipse our thinking unless we recognize them when they come into play and take measures to deal with them. The Child within us may need comfort and reassurance.

Stressful situations heighten the danger of contamination. The fears of the Child in a person at the site of a burning house, for example, may immobilize his Adult and keep him from taking appropriate action. The same thing may happen during a hastily convened staff conference to deal with the latest "fire." Contaminated thinking usually leads to the wrong decision.

Rooted as they are in the past, contaminated thinking and behavior are often inappropriate guides to current action. Supervisors must be particularly careful to avoid such contamination because they make decisions that affect others. They *must* make every effort to be fair and impartial.

part 2:

Hidden levels of communication

People communicate with each other not only to exchange information, but also to reinforce their feelings about themselves and each other. It is at this "feeling" level of communication that they make "transactions" with each other when they communicate. Such transactions on the job are very important. On the one hand, transactions can make people comfortable and free them to work productively; on the other, they can make people uncomfortable and tie up their energy in emotional conflict that renders them almost incapable of working.

The kind of transaction that two people make with each other springs from the particular combination of their respective ego states in action when they communicate. There are three basic kinds of transactions—complementary, crossed, and ulterior.

Complementary transactions

A complementary transaction is one in which the originator gets the kind of response he expects. Let's look at a sample complementary transaction between two supervisors communicating from their Adult ego states:

> *Henry:* "How do you think the merger will affect us?"
> *Carl:* "I think it's too soon to tell."

Henry's remark came from his Adult and sought an Adult response from Carl—which he got. The transaction is thus complementary, and communication is open. Both remarks deal with reality in an objective way.

Consider the following complementary Parent-Parent transaction between supervisors:

> *Frank:* "Those new management trainees think they know it all."
> *Bill:* "Yeah, they're all the same."

The two supervisors, operating from the Critical Parent ego state, are enjoying a good feeling because their Parents have reinforced each other on a shared attitude that they haven't stopped to evaluate. Obviously, the complementary transaction is the one used in giving positive strokes.

Here's a complementary Child-Parent transaction between a harried salesman and his boss:

> *Lou:* "I've got to have some help selling Mac—that tough old bird at the Lakeland account. He stops me cold no matter what I do. Can you help?"
> *Boss:* "Sure, sure. Don't worry about it. I'll go see him."

In this complementary transaction, Lou's Child "hooked" his boss's Nurturing Parent, and Lou got the support he wanted. This kind of support, certainly in large doses, will make Lou dependent.

The next type of transaction, the crossed transaction, occurs when a gambit from one person's ego state draws forth a quite different response from the one expected. As we will see, this tends to stop communication.

Crossed transactions

Let's go back to the merger discussion between supervisors Henry and Carl to show how a different response from Carl can result in a crossed rather than a complementary transaction:

> *Henry:* "How do you think the merger will affect us?"

Carl: "You'd be better off concentrating on your department instead of worrying about the merger. You can't afford to waste any time."

Here, Henry's Adult request for information failed to draw forth an Adult response. Instead, it met with a discount from Carl's Critical Parent. Put-downs like this are all too common on the job—not only because of the competitive spirit in many organizations, but also because our educational system stresses the ability to be critical and evaluative. When we use our highly developed critical faculties inappropriately, we discount other people—making them feel bad. Because crossed transactions can wound people, they can stop or restrict communication and they can destroy the cooperative relations necessary to effective organization functioning.

Let's turn the complementary transaction between salesman Lou and his boss into a crossed one:

Lou: "I've got to have some help selling Mac—that tough old bird at the Lakeland account. He stops me cold no matter what I do. Can you help?"

Boss: "Why does everybody come crying to me with their problems? I have more than enough to do as it is!"

Instead of the expected Parent response, Lou's Child gets a response from his Boss's Child. Both men are complaining; neither is helpful. Both feel discounted.

Maintaining your Adult

If Lou's boss had been familiar with the concepts and techniques of transactional analysis, he might have suspected Lou's gambit to be an attempt to "hook" his Nurturing Parent—and he might have resisted both the hook and an impulse to respond from his Child. Let's look at the situation as Lou's boss might have altered it.

Lou: "I've got to have some help selling Mac—that tough old bird at the Lakeland account. He stops me cold no matter what I do. Can you help?"

Boss: "I think so. Tell me, when do you call on him?"

Lou: "Every Monday morning—and most of the time he won't even see me."

Boss: "It might help you to know that Mac doesn't really warm up to *anything* until after his two martinis with lunch—and on Monday, he warms up more slowly than usual. The best time to call on him is Tuesday or Wednesday afternoon around three o'clock."

What has Lou's boss done here? He has responded to Lou's Child from his Adult. In consciously choosing this course of action, he accomplished two important things: (1) He avoided putting Lou off or stepping in and taking over for him, and (2) his response kept the relationship on an objective basis and gave Lou a chance to try again, this time from his Adult. The persistent use of the Adult in such a situation encourages the other person to do likewise. When this happens, communication is open and it can be productive. Initially, of course, the transaction is crossed. Although there is a possibility that this may stop communication, it is more likely to improve communication if the Adult is used persistently.

Ulterior transactions

The third basic kind of transaction is called ulterior because it involves hidden messages between ego states that are different from the surface or apparent ones. In the following example, Sally's boss is referring to a memo that Sally has already had to retype twice:

Boss: "That's the third draft. It doesn't have to be letter-perfect."

Sally: "I'm finishing it up now."

At first glance, this would seem to be an Adult-Adult transaction. At the surface level it is, but at the psychological level it is a Parent-Child confrontation (as Sally and her boss know very well because they know each other very well). At the hidden level, the transaction goes like this:

Boss: "I'll have to settle for your third draft even if it is messy. Your carelessness is holding everything up."

Sally: "Here's your old draft. I'm tired of being picked on for erasures and minor errors."

Too often, we find it easier to hold our feelings in rather than level with each other. But they find their tortuous way out at the hidden level. Like the crossed transaction, the ulterior transaction can also wound—and cause even greater resentment because the participants aren't being open with each other.

Angular transactions

An angular transaction is a variation of the ulterior transaction. In an angular transaction, the sender's message is deliberately expressed in a way that allows it to appeal to two ego states in the receiver. This is done to manipulate the receiver into a desired course of action. The sender can feel safe because if his attempt at manipulation backfires, he can disclaim it by saying that he was misunderstood. The angular transaction can also be used to sound people out about their feelings and intentions or to get them to say something they may later regret.

Here's an example of how a supervisor maliciously initiates an angular transaction with another supervisor: "I was certainly surprised to hear that you were passed over for promotion. What will you do now?"

Ostensibly an Adult-to-Adult gambit, this comment is designed to draw forth—if possible—a Child response such as, "I'll quit, that's what! *Then* they'll be in the soup." Timed properly, the angular transaction may succeed in eliciting such a response.

True communication is the accurate exchange of meaning and intent among people. The difficulty in achieving it lies in the fact that people hear, see, and understand according to their experiences and their expectations. Because of this, some people view almost all transactions as ulterior. At an early age, they were exposed to many ulterior transactions; their expectations for subsequent transactions were "set." For such people, the meaning of a message often lies more in them than in the sender. Their pasts have overwhelmed them; as a result, they are not reacting realistically to many situations in the present.

Life positions

The way we feel—about ourselves and others—determines to a large extent the kinds of transactions we make with other people, the kinds of strokes we give and seek, the kinds of games we play.

Basically, there are two ways we can feel about other people and ourselves—OK or Not OK. A person who feels OK about himself at heart accepts himself as good and sound. He feels that he is worthwhile as a person, so he doesn't have to spend a great deal of energy trying to demonstrate to others or to himself that he is, in fact, OK. A person feels OK or Not OK from the Child ego state. Typically, this very basic feeling is a carry-over from our formative years. The accumulation of feelings that resulted from early contacts with our parents shaped and hardened

---

A FORMIDABLE INFLUENCE

Your life position has a formidable influence on your relations with other people because it preconditions every encounter you have with others. It will influence, for example, the kinds of jobs you may be successful at; the heights you may achieve; the lengths to which you may go in order *not* to achieve; the company you keep; the number and quality of friendships you enjoy—in short, the quality of your life. Can you think of anything more basic and more consequential in your life than your life position?

---

the way we think and feel toward self and others—a fundamental position transactional analysts call a *life position*. We made this weighty judgement at a time when we were, unfortunately, not up to making it. Unless we later give the matter much thought and make conscious efforts to change it—in some cases, with the help of therapeutic counseling—the position we took back then will continue to govern our actions.

There are four life positions (see below). It is important to recognize the implications of each if we are to account for behavior at work and master our own responses. It should be noted that although these positions operate at a largely unconscious level in maturity, they underlie all our behavior.

THE FOUR LIFE POSITIONS
1. I'm OK—You're OK
2. I'm Not OK—You're OK
3. I'm Not OK—You're Not OK
4. I'm OK—You're Not OK

A person in position Number 1 (I'm OK—You're OK) is a pleasure to everyone concerned. Unlike the other three, which solidify in youth, this position (according to transactional analysts) is finally decided upon in maturity. Herein lies the hope for change through conscious effort by adults who sincerely want to change their lives. The I'm OK—You're OK person is free of the basic hang-ups that result from Not OK feelings; he does not play psychological games. He is prepared to roll up his sleeves and get on with the work. This winner's position allows him to live up to his capabilities and achieve his objectives. He does not have to squander energy on building protective façades, and he does not feel compelled to "check out" the "OKayness" of other people.

Position Number 2 (I'm Not OK—You're OK) is a kind of servile, self-demeaning stance in relation to others. It is a loser's position; the person who holds it feels inferior and is unlikely to attain happiness even if he achieves some success. No matter what happens, it is hard for him to feel good about himself. The pleasure of a recent promotion quickly gives way to anxiety over the next. He is concerned with the approval of others and may work hard to get it. But even this does not bring lasting satisfaction or relief. Because he does not feel good about himself at heart, he finds it difficult to enjoy compliments about himself or his work. His Not OK Child fears failure or rejection and throws up its defenses.

Though he may appear at times to be unconcerned about what others think of him or his work, he really cares a great deal. He may have a tendency to withdraw from others. He needs reassurance and recognition, but most of all he needs a supervisor who demonstrates recognition of his worth as a person apart from his successes or failures. Such an employee can progress well under a supervisor whose predominant style is Nurturing Parent or Adult, but would be completely stunted under a Critical Parent style. Why? Because he would tend to accept Critical Parent rebukes as a true reflection of his personal worth. The best that he would be capable of producing would probably come from his Adapted Child. It would be uninspired, conforming, routine behavior. He would never break out of his shell.

Position Number 3 (I'm Not OK—You're Not OK) is extremely difficult to cope with because it is so negative toward self and others. The employee who holds it may distrust everyone and see little worth in life and work—certainly a loser's position. It would take an extraordinarily sensitive, patient, and understanding supervisor to get through to such a worker. In this as in the other positions there are, of course, degrees of OKayness and not OKayness. Extreme, absolute negativity is fortunately the exception and is treated by professional therapists. Where the position is not extreme, a supervisor can with understanding and patience overcome distrust and build confidence. Such an approach is essential in successful supervision of this kind of person. Some so-called hard-core unemployables may be in this category.

Position Number 4 (I'm OK—You're Not OK) is one in which a person feels good about himself but distrusts and may well look down on others. Such an employee tends to feel superior to others and, to the degree that he does, his supervisor will find it difficult to integrate him into the work team. Though he is likely to be pushy and offensive toward others, he will react indignantly if efforts are made to correct or change him. Since he finds others Not OK, he tends to drive people away. He also tends to come on in his Critical Parent and to offend the Child in others. Paradoxically, he plays the persecutor toward others even though he sees himself as a victim of people out to take advantage of him. However, he may come to accept others on a one-to-one basis after a trial period during which he assures himself that they are not out to "get" him. With such a subordinate, a supervisor must retain his composure at all times and use his Adult and Child appropriately to win the subordinate's respect and allegiance. It is helpful to engage him in Child-Child transactions of the kind that can release tension and build rapport.

The strength of the life positions probably accounts for a great deal of our difficulty in relating to others. Confronted with extreme Not OKayness in a subordinate, we may give up and raise our hands in disgust. The supervisor who has his own Not OK Child to contend with is going to find it difficult to bring about change in employees in life positions Number 3 and Number 4. He will come up short in dealing with Number 3, and he will probably be the object of a good deal of persecution and game playing in situation Number 4.

Fortunately for all of us, these life positions can be reconsidered by the Adult and, with persistence, we can change. We can learn to feel good about ourselves and others and practice new, more appropriate behavior that can make us feel better.

Role playing

Depending upon our inclination to dominate or to be dominated by others, we may be masters of the art of role playing. TA identifies three basic roles—Victim, Persecutor, and Rescuer. Capitalizing these roles indicate that they are parts played in order to manipulate or take advantage of others. There are times when circumstances cast a supervisor in the role of persecutor—for example, when he must fire an employee. And there are times when economic conditions make actual victims of people during plant closedowns and staff reductions. These are distinct from Persecutors and Victims of the role-playing variety who make others suffer needlessly or who seemingly thrive on victimization.

The Rescuer feels impelled to make people dependent on him. He does this by assuming their responsibilities, handling their more difficult assignments, holding back company information they need in order to proceed confidently with their work. He strives to make sure that his people fail to develop their full potential or ever come to realize that they can be successful without him.

Psychological games

Victim, Persecutor, Rescuer—these are the starring roles in psychological game-playing, an important element in the TA approach to understanding behavior. TA game theory hits home for many of us because we have on occasion played psychological games or come up against others who do—even though we may have had no labels for the games and even though we may not have been able to pinpoint precisely what was happening or what was at stake.

Like ordinary games, psychological games offer rewards that motivate players. Unlike ordinary games, most psychological ones are played unconsciously. In both instances, players pass time away, interact, and secure payoffs they value for one reason or another. But the payoff doesn't come in chips, cash, or high numerical tabulations. The payoff is in feelings. Paradoxically, in psychological games "losers" can "win" and "winners" can "lose"—since the object of many such games is to reap or give bad feelings. These games are clearly destructive of good human relations. And since more than two can play simultaneously, human costs to the organization can be staggering.

Psychological game-playing requires skillful, practiced players. To play the games "successfully," people must reliably play out the steps required by their roles. If, for example, the preferred role is Victim, the player knows how to (1) catch the interest of game players who like to play Persecutor or Rescuer, (2) begin a transaction that gives another player (or other players) the opportunity to step in, and (3) know precisely when to alter his behavior in some dramatic way to make the payoff materialize. These skills are usually developed over a period of years, although some people seem to be "naturals."

The "feeling" payoffs can take many forms—anger, increased distrust, disappointment, vengeance, and a heightened sense of superiority or inferiority, to name a few. Employees may use these feelings to get sympathy from others, to hurt them further, or to close or widen the psychological distance between them. By using feelings manipulatively, the game player brings some people under his control and drives others off. A person who sets out—consciously or unconsciously—to satisfy or reinforce Not OK feelings will play games frequently. They become his constant crutch in "getting along" with others.

Games, then, are recurring patterns of behavior fueled by hidden motives. Their salient feature is that *real motives are hidden*. Neither player acknowledges them and, as noted before, neither is usually aware of his precise motives for playing. This is why they can be so devastating to us as decision makers, as people held accountable for the behavior of others.

The effects of hidden feelings

Games certainly make for dishonest relationships—involving, as they do, ulterior motives and hidden feelings. They always result in avoiding authentic contact with others. If the other person is Not OK, how can he be trusted? He can't; he must be kept in his place—at a safe distance. To accomplish this, the game player discounts (abuses, belittles) the other person. The manager who deals in discounts, or negative strokes, must live with the negative consequences that result. These are summarized in the box on page 26.

Note that the "I'm OK" aspect of a life position is resistant to discounting. For the person with this basic feeling, a discounting manager is sim-

EFFECTS OF REPEATED DISCOUNTING

If the Employee's Life Position is:	Discounting May Result in:
I'm OK—You're OK	Modifying it to I'm OK—You're Not OK
I'm OK—You're Not OK	Confirming this position
I'm Not OK—You're Not OK	Confirming this position
I'm Not OK—You're OK	Modifying it to I'm Not OK—You're Not OK

ply proving that *he's* Not OK. However, OK—Not OK positions are seldom absolute in the sense that *all* other people are seen as Not OK or that they are seen as 100 percent Not OK. OKayness is a matter of degree, and we make exceptions—so another person's standing with us is subject to change, for better or worse.

In view of the effects of discounting, it is obviously wise to confine reprimands to a subordinate's undesirable *behavior* and avoid attacking him as a person. That is, instead of saying "You are this and you are that and therefore you are not acceptable to me," your approach should be "Doing this or doing that is not acceptable to me." Similarly, the old guidelines of disciplining in private and praising in public still hold water.

Even though the price tag on game-playing behavior may be very high, games go on because they are usually unconscious; they satisfy a basic need to fill time in a way that reinforces life positions, thus reassuring the player that he is "alive and well"; they bring rewards in the form of feelings that the player collects. Gamesters associate with other gamesters, of course, and many games complement each other. For example, an employee who plays STUPID, KICK ME, and other Victim-oriented games may well be found working for a supervisor who enjoys his role in such Persecutor games as NIGYSOB (to be explained later in detail).

Just as there are degrees of OKayness and Not OKayness, so are there degrees of acceptability among games. The games played by most people at work are mild in comparison with games involving costly payoffs— games that may end, as Eric Berne noted, in courtrooms, jailcells, and morgues.

Let's take a look at some specific games played on the job. A supervisor, like an employee, may be drawn into them without realizing it—

NIGYSOB

The game called NIGYSOB ("Now I've Got You, You S.O.B.") results in confirming the player's conviction that the respondent is unreliable. The payoff is a discount for the respondent, who typically plays such complementary games as STUPID and KICK ME.

Mark, who runs a large warehouse stocked with various home furnishings, likes to play NIGYSOB. He runs the warehouse like a martinet, setting impossible goals for his subordinates and then indulging himself in angry explosions when they fail to measure up. Mark often operates from his Critical Parent—and the subordinates who have stayed with him reciprocate with their Adapted Child. Here's a sample NIGYSOB game between Mark and his assistant:

Mark: "What's the inventory level now on Number 603 red floor tile—not counting the orders that have been received but not filled yet?"

Assistant: "Well, I don't know exactly. It's turning over fast because headquarters gave it a 15 percent discount. It's somewhere between 25 and 27 cases. I'll know more exactly when I hear from the eastern salesmen. They . . ."

Mark: "Don't give me any excuses! I want up-to-the minute inventory counts—and you know it! If you can't keep up with them, find a job that's better suited to your mentality!"

Obviously, Mark's life position is I'm OKay—You're Not OKay, one in which his assistant concurs. Actually, Mark's assistant could simply have replied "26 cases" to Mark's question, but that would have stopped the game short of a payoff.

When Mark fails to set up a NIGYSOB game, his assistant initiates a KICK ME game—and, of course, Mark obliges. Despite the frequency with which they play and "win," they are both losers in the long run—and the warehouse suffers, too.

BLEMISH

In the following example, a supervisor with a You're Not OK life position is out to drive his point home with an employee who doesn't concur with his boss's position toward him. The name of the game is BLEMISH.

Supervisor: "Harry, how soon can you get me a runoff of the payroll breakdown?"

Harry: "I have it here. See—it includes the latest column refinements."

Supervisor: "Wait a minute. What's that?"

Harry: "Just a spacing error."

Supervisor: "Just a spacing error! This is intolerable!"

Harry: "But it doesn't change the report in any way."

Supervisor: "That doesn't matter. You ought to know better than to try to get away with slipshod work like this."

This is a game the boss always "wins." If the subordinate strenuously objects, the boss could persecute him more vigorously and escalate the situation into a game called UPROAR. Then they would trade abuses that would lead to extreme behavior. Someone might throw a punch. Someone might be fired. Even if the payoff isn't final, each can take pleasure in knowing that he was absolutely right in what he did. Why, he must have had the other person pegged right from the very start.

YES, BUT

A popular game around the office is YES, BUT. It may be played as follows:

Carol: "I'd like you to do an article on training for the company newsletter."

George: "I wish I could help you, but I'm awfully busy on this project."

Carol: "Mr. Farrell told me you could put it aside."

George: "Yes, but if I did that I'd never meet the deadline."

Carol: "I'll get some temporary help for you."

George: "The last thing I need is those dumb temporary people who don't know which end is up."

Carol: "You can show them how you want things done."

George: "Yes, but if I do that I won't have any time to do your article."

As you can see, the game can be carried on to impressive heights of absurdity. Although the voiced level of communication is mostly on an Adult-Adult basis, at the hidden level a Parent-Child transaction is in progress. Carol is coming on Parent, trying to give instruction and help to George's stubborn Child. George's Child is replying, in effect, "Nothing you say is going to influence me." It takes considerable skill to contend with master game players who have refined their craft through long practice.

A related game is WHY DON'T YOU . . . YES, BUT. In it, the hidden Parent-Child transactions are more evident. Supervisors and others who have a tendency to advise people or play Rescuer find themselves on the WHY DON'T YOU end of the game. Heres a sample game in progress:

Supervisor: "How are you doing at night school?"

Employee: "Not well; it's too time consuming."

Supervisor: "Why don't you take fewer courses?"

Employee: "Yes, I could do that—but it would take so much longer to complete the program."

Supervisor: "Why don't you reduce the course load by spreading it out? You could attend during the summer."

Employee: "Yes, but if I did that I wouldn't have time for my family."

Supervisor: "Well, you could arrange your courses during the school year so that you attend only one night per week."

Employee: "Yes, but that would mean using up my electives in taking courses that I don't want."

Supervisor: "Why don't you. . . ."

The game goes on and on nonproductively, with each player trying to best the other, as in a contest of wits. Playing such games is not only an insecure way for people to relate to each other, but can also be extremely time consuming and costly to management.

Another on-the-job game is the AIN'T IT AWFUL game. Like other games, this one is nonproductive—even though positive stroking rather than discounting is involved. In the following example, Hank is playing AIN'T IT AWFUL with a fellow supervisor who is in the habit of playing it with him.

Hank: "You try to do a job around here and what do you get?"

Fellow supervisor: "I know what you mean; it's awful."

Hank: "I don't know why I put up with it."

Fellow supervisor: "They're incapable of appreciating good work and dedication."

Hank: "You'd think they'd change their ways before it's too late."

Fellow supervisor: "They wouldn't know how to."

Does this dialogue resolve or change anything? No. Despite the shared joy of a mutual Parent attitude, Hank does not learn from his experience, and his companion has not shed light on anything.

AIN'T IT AWFUL lends itself to team operations. Too often, task forces or committees authorized to study problems and make recommendations for action forsake analysis of the problems in favor of going on a Parent-Parent binge. Much time is spent expressing concern, regret, and disgust —but nothing is done. The members never come to grips with root problems. Their collective Adult waits its turn while the Parents play their

AN EMPLOYEE ... When His Life Position Is:	Communicates	Accepts Delegation	Develops	Handles Disagreement	Solves Problems	Spends Time	Is Moved to Act	Feels Toward Others
I'M OK – YOU'RE OK	Openly	Readily	Independently, Learns Willingly	By Seeking Clarification and Mutual Resolution	By Consulting Others, Trusting Himself	Taking Necessary Action and Producing	On Assignment or Initiative	Equal
I'M NOT OK – YOU'RE OK	Defensively Self-Deprecatingly	Timidly	Slowly; Needs Reassurance and Coaching	By Perceiving Differences in Opinion as Evidence of His Inadequacy	By Relying Almost Completely on Others	Brooding or Overcompensating in Constant Activity	By Praise or Admonition	Inferior
I'M OK – YOU'RE NOT OK	Defensively Aggressively	By Procrastinating, Bickering, and Bargaining	With Difficulty; Learning Is Blocked	By Placing Blame on Others	By Unilaterally Rejecting Others' Ideas	Boasting, Provoking Others, Playing Persecutor	When Forced; May Demand Official Instructions	Superior
I'M NOT OK – YOU'RE NOT OK	Hostilely Abruptly	By Trying to Beg Off, Delegating Upward. Unwillingly Accepts Responsibility	With Difficulty; Withdraws and Repeats Errors	By Escalating the Conflict; Involving a Third Party	By Succumbing to Problems	Withdrawing; Playing a Variety of Games	By Reprimands or Threats	Despondent Alienated

HOW LIFE POSITION INFLUENCES EMPLOYEE BEHAVIOR

game. An infrequency and low-level intensity of game playing certainly are good indications of an organization's health.

Understanding games and their effects

To understand game playing, the supervisor must (1) note the kinds of feelings collected as payoffs and (2) watch the frequency with which players play. Once a supervisor identifies games, he can begin to reduce their frequency and intensity. A good place to begin is with one's own behavior. The questions to ask here are: "Am I easily hooked into other people's games? Do I repeatedly do things that bring on bad feelings? Do I insist upon advising or rebuking people even when no good will come of it? Do I seize every opportunity to get back at 'offenders'?" A supervisor must use his Adult to mediate his actions in such matters. If he does not, he is likely to become hunter or prey in unceasing games.

How do people who work for a game-playing supervisor behave? Usually, they respond either by learning to play the games involved, or by withdrawing and becoming passive. In an effort to protect themselves from persecution that they don't understand and can't attribute to their own behavior, subordinates usually resort to defensive reporting. An employee who feels victimized may decide that the safest route to survival is to:

- Tell the boss what he wants to hear, even if it's a lie.
- Tell him no more than what he specifically asks for.
- Tell him nothing that can lead to punishment.

The supervisor whose behavior triggers these reactions is self-defeating, because timely, accurate, complete information is the lifeblood of organizations. Moreover, such supervisory behavior exemplifies the phenomenon called the "self-fulfilling prophecy": The supervisor involved acts in a way that brings forth undesirable behavior he had predicted in his subordinates at the outset. In other words, treat a subordinate as though he can't be trusted, and soon he will become untrustworthy. Treat him as though he has no initiative, and he will fulfill your expectation.

How games are halted: It takes two to play

Since games are played to obtain payoffs, the best thing a supervisor can do to stop one is to withhold the payoff. Half a transaction does not make a game. If an employee is playing KICK ME, don't kick him. That just reinforces his behavior. Instead, use your Adult in calling upon him to use his Adult to change his behavior. Persistence in using your Adult can get him to recognize the deficiency of his behavior and commit himself to changing it.

Don't, however, tell him that you think he is playing a psychological game. He may not understand and will resent your psychologizing. Even if he does understand, he's not likely to admit to anything. Disclosure may even strengthen his resolve to play games. If you lose your perspective and come on with your Critical Parent, you provide the expected payoff and continue the game. If the game is STUPID, refuse to imply that you think him stupid. You can expect a tough struggle with your own Critical Parent in this—but you must center on the *behavior* of the person, not his personal attributes, whatever they may be.

When you separate the person from the act, his Not OK feelings will diminish because you are neither reinforcing nor threatening his self-concept. Your relationship will be one in which you can respect and stroke the person and continue to expect behavioral change for the better. Games can be ended only by an Adult determination to find other, more genuine ways to get along. In the same manner, life positions can be changed to I'm OK—You're OK. These changes do not come easily. They have to be worked at in an environment that makes it possible for people to grow and develop. ∎

part 3:
Styles of supervision

Leadership styles have been characterized by the use of numbered grids, behavior scales or continuums, and such various terms as autocrat, benevolent autocrat, joiner, quarterback, seller, and bureaucrat. Describing them in TA terms can shed some light on the way we use our ego states in leadership situations. Where a style is not working for a supervisor because his predominant ego state tends to put people off or put them down, he can change it by appropriately using other ego states more often. A knowledge of TA style possibilities makes change easier. The only caution here is that in using behavior from other ego states, the supervisor must be sincere. To be otherwise would be manipulative. It would be "playing a role"—and, in the end, he would find himself less effective than before.

Style, for our purposes, is "the way a supervisor relates to his employees in getting a job done and in meeting overall objectives." A supervisor's style shows in how he gets others to perform, how he gets along with others, and how he interprets his responsibilities. Style change should be undertaken only after a careful analysis of the ways

PARENT    ADULT    CHILD

in which he relates to others and the ways in which others expect him to behave. The nature of the work being performed, of course, should also be taken into account. The idea is to become aware of the style he is using and the impact of that style on the effective management of others. Take a look at the following style classifications, which are based on the use of a predominant ego state.

The Natural Child supervisor

The Natural Child supervisor too often uses the inappropriate and least admirable traits of the Child ego state. He is selfish, and he is not committed to furthering the goals either of subordinates or of the organization. His behavior ranges from being chummy with subordinates to withdrawal and passivity to occasional outbursts or temper tantrums when he is criticized for not performing. Although he easily makes friends with one or two subordinates (by appealing to their Child), he blatantly plays favorites and stirs up resentment in doing so. Moreover, he can with equal ease alienate the one or two friends he does make. He does not recognize or admit that he is particularly ineffective and usually responds to such charges by pointing out behavior in colleagues that he feels is going unnoticed by higher management. He claims that he is being singled out for critical treatment—and he makes this feeling known even to those who work for him. As a result, his subordinates lose respect for him and the organization; they may take advantage of a situation in which they are not required to produce.

This kind of supervisor is obviously not effective as a leader. Good performers leave him at the first opportunity. Ineffective subordinates remain with him or gravitate toward him—giving his department a reputation for being a kind of limbo for people in transit or on their way out. Important work is shifted from him to other supervisors—who often resent having to accommodate it. They feel that they are being burdened because of higher management's unwillingness to confront him with his shortcomings. Such a supervisor saps the vitality of the organization in several ways. First, because others have to salvage work that he began, he is responsible for a situation in which nonperformance is rewarded and performance is punished. The other supervisors who do the salvage work resent this situation. And the same resentment permeates working levels, where it is expressed in discontent with which other supervisors must deal.

No positive strokes come from this supervisor. He tends to use crooked and very conditional strokes in his dealings with others. He puts across the message, "I'll like you *if* . . ." (you do things exactly my way, you make me look good to my boss, you cater to my personal whims, etc.). His games, which are an important part of his existence, tend to be of the "If it weren't for (you)" variety. Employees seeking guidance or coaching from him generally find themselves in crossed transactions. They address him on an Adult-to-Adult basis, but he responds irresponsibly from his Child.

Further characteristics

This supervisor tends to maintain an I'm Not OK—You're Not OK life position. He is variously aloof, frenetically playful, indecisive, unconcerned, uncommitted, whining, selfish, and complaining. Making a decision is anathema to him. Just as his favorite role is Victim, his favorite associates are other Victims and Rescuers. Motto: "Why don't they get off my back?" Games played: WHY DOES THIS ALWAYS HAPPEN TO ME? KICK ME, STUPID, AIN'T IT AWFUL, IF IT WEREN'T FOR. . . .

The Critical Parent supervisor

The Critical Parent supervisor wants and insists upon maximum production, but seldom gets it. Although his chief means of communicating with others is Critical Parent to Child, he may use Nurturing Parent behavior in a last-ditch attempt at manipulation. People see through him easily, and they resent being treated as children who can't be trusted to be responsible for their own behavior. Using threats and intimidation to get his way, he frequently puts people down and seldom can bring himself to give praise or other rewards for performance. He resents being so seldom stroked himself, and seems to operate on the assumption that he and everyone else must constantly prove themselves acceptable as human beings. Any positive stroking on his part is brief, very conditional (given only when his exacting standards are met), and frequently diluted: "Not a bad job, considering. . . ."

His subordinates feel that no matter what they do, no matter how hard they work, there is no pleasing him. His behavior fosters emotional and intellectual dependency—with the result that people find it difficult to grow and develop under him. His style attracts people with Not OK Child feelings to work for him. He creates an atmosphere in which they can play games that confirm their Not OK feelings.

Further characteristics

This supervisor handles conflict by oppressive means; the direction of his communication is primarily downward and one-way. His favorite role is Persecutor, which fits his I'm OK—You're Not OK life position. Motto: "I'll do the thinking. You do what you're told." Games played: BLEMISH, CORNER, NOW I'VE GOT YOU, YOU S.O.B.

The Nurturing Parent supervisor

The Nurturing Parent supervisor strokes people unconditionally for being people—because he likes them and wants to be liked in return. The trouble is that he tolerates minimal performance and usually pitches in to help the work along. Self-motivated achievers may fare well with him if they themselves provide the initiative necessary to forge ahead —to grow personally and professionally on the job. Things tend to remain static in his department even though morale for most people in his rather close work group is high. If the supervisor is a true rescuer, people can and will develop in his organization. After all, he does value such development, and he knows it doesn't happen accidentally. But his subordinates will develop slowly in a minimum-risk, low-key atmosphere.

If he's a role-playing Rescuer, it's important for him to maintain their dependence upon him. He may even set people up to fail and afterwards lull them into continued dependence. He will play games to the extent necessary to achieve these results. Whenever possible, he will create an image for subordinates that he alone stands between them and a hard-crusted, insensitive management. This is to ensure that they will value him all the more.

Further characteristics

This supervisor tends to have an I'm OK—You're Not OK life position, and the primary direction of his communication is downward. The honest rescuer type of Nurturing Parent has this motto: "Don't worry about things. We'll work them out." The manipulatory Rescuer takes a different tack: "What would you do without me?" Games played include I'M ONLY TRYING TO HELP YOU and LET'S YOU AND HIM FIGHT.

The Adapted Child supervisor

The chief concern of the Adapted Child supervisor is to perform precisely to the minimal degree necessary. A foot-dragger who has to be badgered into better performance, he seeks acceptance from everyone. As a result, he hesitates to go all out or to innovate. He exercises great skill to avoid offending anyone and may use his Manipulative Child to assure his aims. Because he has trouble unleashing his Natural Child, he lacks creativity and joy in achievement.

This supervisor is the product of organizations or supervisors who discount innovative, aggressive behavior. Over a period of time, he has developed a compulsion to secure his status through carefully prescribed behavior. He tends to be conservative, accepting of others, and upward-oriented in his needs for dependency. Faced with a decision that he feels may be unpopular, he will try to delegate it upward. If this fails, he will probably procrastinate, hoping that the problem will go away if he waits it out. He has a tendency to be apologetic and defensive. When things get tough, he starts buck-passing and fault-finding.

Further characteristics

The primary direction of this supervisor's communication is upward. Because he is heavily dependent for his inner security upon authority figures and their estimate of his work (and worth), he tends to behave as though he has an "I'm OK *if*—You're OK *if* . . . life position. At all costs he will avoid organizational and interpersonal conflict. Games played: SEE WHAT YOU MADE ME DO, IF IT WEREN'T FOR. . . .

The Adult supervisor

The Adult supervisor is not one who always acts from his Adult ego state. Rather, he uses his Adult to filter and assemble his thoughts before he acts. Then, when he does act, it's in a way appropriate to the needs of the situation. He may act from any of his ego states, but he will do so only after consulting his Adult. He can supervise a broad range of employees effectively. He is as much concerned about them as persons as he is with getting a job done well.

Because this supervisor can communicate with people on a variety of levels, he is a good motivator and team builder; he can deal well with individuals or groups. He knows when to joke and how to empathize with others, and he finds it easy to be candid with people. When rewards are in order, he has no difficulty in stroking subordinates. People like him because he is capable of accepting them as they are while urging them on to further growth and development. He does not play roles. He does not "put on." He levels with his people and asks that they do so with him. People feel free to approach him because they know from experience that he will not put them down or put them off.

He does not foster dependency, but encourages people to deal with problems from their Adult. He is a good delegator, a supervisor who expects each person to perform to the degree to which he is capable. His is possibly the only style of supervision in which deliberately straight strokes (good feelings, rewards) are commonly and honestly given.

Further characteristics

Such a supervisor has an I'm OK—You're OK life position. His motto: "Together, we can do almost anything." He does not manipulate others, and he does not play games.

The supervisory styles described above are not likely to exist in such extreme, pure states. Like everyone, supervisors have three ego states; their behavior should shift from one state to another according to the demands of the situation and their best interpretation of what is appropriate behavior for effective supervision under the circumstances. However, taking a look at these styles in their pure states should make it easier for a supervisor to understand the sources of his behavior.

Many supervisors have a favorite or habitual style based primarily on use of one or two of the styles discussed. A style is good to the degree that it lends itself to the accomplishment of objectives and produces satisfying human relations. If either is lacking, some change is in order. Change can start with more concern for people or more concern for getting work done, or both.

A supervisor who habitually uses the Critical Parent to meet objectives does so at a high cost to the people who work for him—and to the productivity of his department. Change for him will mean more trusting, more nurturing behavior toward others. He will have to delegate more fully and reward performance if he is to be more effective. His supervisory practices will have to aim at developing rather than at discounting people. If he recognizes himself as a psychological game player, he will need to stop his games and learn to derive satisfaction from authentic, straightforward transactions. When he learns to stroke employees as people as well as for what they do, he will be well on the way to improving his effectiveness.

There is no ideal supervisory profile—though some are obviously better than others. Neither is there one "real" ego state. All of them are "real" in the sense that they are different presentations appropriate to different environments. Most people can and do alter their behavior in different circumstances. Some people, however, do not. Their rigid behavior stems from their almost exclusive use of Parent, Adult, or Child. On a day-to-day basis in a single setting—such as work—supervisors do tend to present themselves in a habitual way. This is why there is value in studying styles. When a supervisor's style becomes rigid, his effectiveness diminishes. ■

part 4:
Motivation and counseling

Motivation and counseling are two of the best methods a supervisor has for raising employee productivity and performance levels. Let's take a look first at motivation and then at counseling to see the ways in which TA techniques can increase the effectiveness with which a supervisor uses these methods.

Motivation in the TA sense requires consideration of each ego state to encourage a worker to reach departmental goals. The highest level of motivation flourishes in a job where he or she can get strokes for all three ego states. Remember that a worker who is unable to find satisfactory positive strokes from the job for his Parent, Adult, and Child won't hesitate to disrupt work to get any kind of strokes at all from you or from his co-workers.

He may, for example, play KICK ME with you, BLEMISH with a younger worker, or AIN'T IT AWFUL with a peer. All stroke searches of this nature are counterproductive. Whether a worker goes after a put-down from you or indulges in Parent-Parent binges with his peers, he wastes hours of his own and others' time.

But, you may say, do I really have to pay attention to the Parent, Adult, and Child of every subordinate? That triples my staff! The answer is *yes*—do so selectively and appropriately, and you will also increase efficiency or output. Take the Parent ego state, for example. Parent tapes contain many, many messages concerning what work we do, what satisfaction it gives, what values should be placed on various kinds of work, what constitutes fair treatment at work, what obligations employees have to employers (and vice versa), and other work-related opinions and values. By satisfying an employee's Parent, a supervisor releases his energy from internal conflict—making it available for productive activity.

Different strokes for different folks

Satisfying a particular employee's Parent requires some preliminary observation. You may notice, for example, that a worker with a very critical Parent makes concessions to it through excessive work—when he doesn't, he loses his peace of mind. Another employee's Critical Parent may demand competitiveness at all times; still another's may dictate that the worker must feel a sense of purpose and satisfaction in working. Thus, Parent tapes may require a wide range of commitment to work as such—from very little to a great deal. The degree of commitment involved will inevitably determine the measures necessary to motivate a subordinate. Some, for example, may never be satisfied in the work they are doing; attempts to enrich their work by making it more challenging, difficult, or responsible merely turn them off. On the whole, though, job enrichment has proved a success—in part, at least, because many people please their Parent by valuing things the Parent values; our society is, after all, still a work- and achievement-oriented one.

Enriching his job usually satisfies a worker's Parent because it allows him to assume more responsibility for his actions, to achieve more, to become more productive—in short, to *make good*. The effect of this is to help reduce interior conflict between Parent and Child. The Parent admonition to the Child—"You should do more with your life"—is answered by the Adult: "My employer recognizes this; I am being given more responsibility and authority." This brings self-approval and relaxes tensions. The desire to do and be more fuels the upward-mobility aspirations of many workers today.

For the Adult, the sense of challenge that comes of being entrusted to do a difficult job is an important motivator. When an employee must stretch to do a little more than he thought possible, he will not only grow with success, but enjoy a sense of renewed confidence in his Adult capability. Additionally, he receives strokes from his supervisor in the form of praise and recognition—very rewarding in themselves. The realization that he can think on his own feet, that he can handle himself well in a demanding situation, makes him feel good. Increased attention to a job's "thinking" requirements, always an important consideration in enriching a job, involves giving a subordinate a variety of stimulating and more difficult tasks. The fact that it calls on him to share in decisions affecting his work exercises his Adult and reassures his Parent.

Taking care of the Child

Since the Child is the primary source of our feelings about ourselves, the work we are given to do must strengthen its sense of OKayness. This comes of being able to succeed, not by experiencing repeated failures. A series of failures can result, for example, when a person is developed too rapidly or is underqualified for what he is doing. An employee with Not OK feelings about himself will also be frustrated and held back by a supervisor whose behavior is largely Critical Parent. Of course, this is in general true for everyone. But it is likely to have a sharper, more permanent impact on the development of employees who are least prepared to cope with such an unfortunate experience. The supervisor who tends to "come on" with his Critical Parent may not tolerate mistakes in learning or may expect too much or too little. Unless both supervisor and worker draw upon more Adult behavior, their relationship will remain a one-way situation, leaving the employee a passive recipient, a puppet on a string. The ultimate consequences will be psychological game playing and/or withdrawal. Once an employee withdraws, he moves beyond the reach of job enrichment or any other form of motivation; he stops growing in his job. The opposite occurs when the supervisor has an effective style of leadership. Then the employee moves from withdrawal toward involvement, increasing his sense of OKayness.

On any job, the Child is the source of creativity. For its creativity to grow or even remain functional, the Child needs to exercise its abundant curiosity. Many job activities lend themselves to the exercise of creativity. The roots of work simplification, for example, develop in a creative frame of mind that permits fresh viewpoints or novel thinking about traditional methods. Creative thinking facilitates almost any kind of planning and problem-solving.

Few people would question the value of being able to produce a lot of ideas or alternatives. Brainstorming groups make exclusive use of each member's Child in order to produce a lot of ideas. This technique absolutely forbids criticism or critical thinking on the part of any member's Parent or Adult while the group is working to generate ideas. Only after a sufficient quantity of new ideas emerges does the group begin to use the collective Adult to evaluate them objectively.

The Child is also the affectionate part of the personality that can make it easier for people to get together and build friendships. When we separate people who are part of a strong informal group—perhaps by erecting cubicles around them—these relationships suffer and morale often drops. People need to socialize and share feelings on a Child-Child friendship basis. Modern motivational programs recognize this by forming work groups based on common tasks or assembly operations and locating people in physical proximity to each other. The need to socialize is quite strong in some people; many consider job friendships to be a primary source of satisfaction in employment. Such people may find it intolerable to work for a supervisor who is unable to express feelings from his Child —who forever comes on all Parent or all Adult. His psychological distance disturbs them.

It's important to remember that people want to be liked as well as accepted and utilized properly. Between any two people, the greater the number of communication paths between their ego states, the longer lived and more satisfactory their relationship is likely to be. That is, when they are both "cooking on all burners," their common interests let them enjoy good rapport. If a breakdown occurs on one level, others are open. In a large hierarchical organization, incidentally, such mutually satisfactory relationships promote efficiency in getting work done despite barriers that the organizational structure may erect. The same, of course, holds true within smaller working groups. In an environment where people have no rapport with each other, one danger is that they will turn their creativity against the organization or against each other in self-defeating conflict.

It's clear, then, that the supervisor who would motivate subordinates must appeal to—must "deal" in—feelings. One way to see clearly how feelings are used and abused is to think of them as trading stamps like the ones you can get when you buy something at certain stores. When you get them, you can either redeem them quickly for a small item that strikes your fancy or you can save them up until you have enough to get something "big."

Stamps of all colors

We use feelings in much the same way. Because we do, TA compares feelings to trading stamps. Muriel James and Dorothy Jongeward have identified blue stamps for depression, brown for feeling inadequate, white for blamelessness, red for anger, gold for good feelings. We all collect feelings in our contacts with others. We collect such stamps at work, at home, everywhere we go. Like trading stamps, they can be cashed in on the spot, or we can save them up to fill a few stampbooks. We can choose to express our feelings when they are small, and get them out of our system, or we can let them pile up until we explode at someone. Turning in an accumulation of red stamps can be quite costly—when, for example, we "take it out" on subordinates, pounce on the secretary, give the boss what he has coming, tell personnel what the company can do with the job, etc.

Listening has long been touted as an important social skill for any manager because it allows subordinates to ventilate such feelings (turn in their stamp collection) while the feelings, or collections, are still small. The manager who listens effectively accepts the expression of feelings because he knows that they are not something to be held in contempt or to be ashamed of. In fact, he wants to contend with them early on, because he knows that if he ignores them, he'll only find them expressed in some distorted form later on.

Let them collect gold stamps

Supervisors interested in motivating subordinates through the job or work afford every opportunity for them to collect gold stamps on the job. By doing work that is rewarding for their Parent, Adult, and Child ego states, they collect good feelings. When their supervisor further strokes or rewards them for the good work they do, their self-confidence and sense of OKayness increases—more gold stamps—and their proficiency increases apace. Briefly, the two primary sources of gold stamps are satisfaction from doing the job and recognition for doing the job well. The resulting good feelings reinforce the actions that produced them and lead to still higher levels of performance.

Reinforcement: actions and feelings

A supervisor's motivation efforts, then, should center on getting a subordinate started in an upward spiral where feelings and actions reinforce each other. Lacking job satisfaction and recognition, the subordinate's growth stops—he is not able to reach any kind of self-fulfillment through job performance. People who are dissatisfied with their work collect red, blue, and brown stamps—which lead nowhere in terms of employee development. These negative feelings accumulate by the "bookful" and result in serious consequences. Here are a few of the ways in which they find expression:

- Employee game-playing and conflicts develop.
- Manhours are wasted.
- Products/services deteriorate.
- Customer relations turn sour.
- The production of constructive ideas withers away.

Put simply, Not OK feelings toward self and others increase, and the work place becomes an exchange center for negative feelings. Have you ever worked with someone who collected blue stamps every day? You probably collected a few just by being near that person. Each of us has a favorite color in our stamp collection. We collect more of some colors than others and, again, the sizes of our collections vary.

When we're under a lot of pressure, we collect and cash in stamps more rapidly as our Adult is "squeezed." Under great pressure—for example, in a tough, short-fused project where error could result in the loss of a job, a promotion, or a customer—we may become so disoriented that we fail. That is, under such pressure, old tapes may take over our thinking. We feel anxious, confused, and angry at ourselves. The Parent steps in with a barrage of such critical remarks as: "You should have been better prepared for this." "If you had trained your people better, you wouldn't be in this mess." "You never were much of a planner." The Child sulks, worries and feels inadequate: "I know I'm going to fail." "This is too much for me." "It isn't fair." "Maybe I'm in the wrong line of work." "Maybe I ought to quit." Meanwhile, the Adult is hard put even to get a thought in. There is simply no computer time available. It's easy to see the possibilities for stamp collecting here. Under the circumstances, we're ready to accept as valid any negative stroke being dished out.

Feeling rackets

A word of caution for the supervisor who is affecting and being affected by the feelings of other employees: Watch out for racketeers! A racketeer is a person who exploits others in some illegitimate, covert way in order to satisfy his own selfish ends. A feeling racketeer does essentially the same thing. It is one thing to be a feeling, responding person who is subject to real anger, joy, and other legitimate emotions—but it is quite another to seek out bad feelings in order to manipulate people. The term *feeling racket* applies to the way in which a person zaps others or maneuvers them to zap *him* (not necessarily consciously) so that he can manipulate them by playing Persecutor or Victim. Gamesters do this all the time. They take measures to exaggerate "the grief that others cause them" and they look to others for sympathy.

A manager must be able to differentiate between feelings that are appropriate to what has gone on and those that are distorted. He'll have to use his Adult to find out when an employee's collected stamps are real and when they are just figments of the imagination. Many people get into habits of collecting certain feelings, of course, because doing so helps confirm their life positions. Some seem to need to feel guilty, or without fault, or righteous in their "martyrdom." People who get satisfaction from such feelings are said to be in a feeling racket.

Now, you could say that such people are motivated. They certainly are —to achieving ulterior goals! But these goals are not in the best interest of the individual or the organization as a whole. To leave the way clear for productive motivation, we need to learn to make "computer time" for the Adult—i.e., give the Adult a chance to operate. And we need to start exchanging gold stamps. The supervisor who is able to give gold stamps and stimulate others to give and collect them will ultimately be able to build them into a solid currency in his department. By and large, the emphasis will be on good feelings through honest, aboveboard transactions. Only in such an atmosphere can workers feel free to achieve their highest potential.

Counseling

Even under conditions that yield high motivation, however, an occasional worker may for one reason or another have trouble achieving high performance. The trouble may lie in inadequate training, a poor fit between his skills and his job, a seemingly intractable personality conflict, or some other reason. Whatever the reason, you must step in with counseling to alleviate the trouble—and TA techniques can help you do so effectively.

Counseling from the TA viewpoint is a series of transactions designed to improve performance, solve a personal or job-related problem, or develop a path for growth and development. The counseling interview is used to solicit and exchange information, thoughts, and feelings bearing on a problem situation.

TA techniques help broaden our understanding of the important internal events that underlie such encounters. Through transactional analysis, we learn to deal with emotions as well as thoughts—a procedure crucial to successful counseling. During a counseling interview, you have to deal with your own Parent, Adult, and Child as well as those of the employee.

The authority relationship between you and your subordinate poses certain difficulties for some kinds of counseling transactions. There is, for example, the continuing danger that the supervisor's Parent may come on heavy—dominating, intimidating, or patronizing the employee. When this happens, the employee is likely to be frightened or enticed into responding exclusively from his Child—thereby preventing any constructive Adult involvement or commitment. "Whatever you say" replaces "Try to see it from my point of view"—and the interview fails. The supervisor must become aware of his prevailing way of interacting with the employee so that he can take any necessary measures to activate his Adult. On the other hand, he may be *so* Adult-oriented that he seems personally unconcerned and aloof—a position guaranteed to produce a sterile interchange. Let's examine TA's role in the counseling process.

Before the interview

Before a counseling interview, the supervisor will use his time wisely by informing his Adult of necessary facts and considerations. In addition, he may want to examine any Parent or Child programming he has that may make him critical toward the employee or cause him distress in dealing with the employee. By surfacing any anxiety or prejudice involved, he will strengthen his Adult for the task ahead. After this internal review, the Adult can prepare for the interview by examining external files and records that apply.

Knowing the employee's typical response patterns will also help. Consider how you will deal with the employee who has a Not OK view of himself or of you. Be prepared to establish the rapport so necessary in counseling and anticipate ways of getting around any sore points that may interfere with your transactions. Having done these things, you can define your objectives for the counseling interview. If it is intended to change employee behavior, you should have a clear image of how the employee will act after his behavior changes. Define yardsticks for measuring success. Ask yourself, "How will I know when the problem is solved—for him, for me?" "What will things be like at that time?" We often act without an answer to these questions. Trying to answer them will help you spot areas of your ignorance, possible prejudices, wishful thinking, and just plain ill-considered objectives.

If you have a tendency to play Rescuer, ask yourself whether this is truly in the employee's interest. A primary counseling goal is to help the employee stand on his own two feet, to use his Adult successfully. Are you prepared for this to happen? Do you really want this to happen? Check out your "rescuing" motivation. Is it real, or are you doing it merely for personal aggrandizement? One game played by manipulative Rescuers is called "I'm Only Trying to Help You." If you suspect yourself of being this kind of gamester, you might prepare your Child so that it won't be offended when your advice isn't accepted. The best preventive measure, however, is simply to refrain from giving advice. People rarely want or follow outside advice that they haven't internalized to their own satisfaction. What you really want to do is to get the employee to be responsible for his own actions. You are successful when you help him to be his own rescuer. This process is called employee development.

The interview

To put the employee at ease, start by engaging him in a short period of discussion about things that interest him. You can relax his Child by being open and friendly and by announcing the purpose of the interview. Taking an informal tone of voice and posture also helps. Arms folded across chest, hands tinkering with something on the desk, a vacant, distinterested stare, etc., will put him off. Some supervisors establish a better basis for rapport by moving out from behind their desks to align themselves closer with the employee. The following list of do's and don'ts are designed to help you take it from there.

• <u>Don't try to change his/her personality.</u> You can't change the content of the employee's ego states. You *can* help him to become aware of their content and elicit his Adult response in mediating his thinking and behavior. Once you do this, you're practically home free.

• <u>Hold your Parent and Child in check.</u> Don't fall into a closed Parent-Child transaction in which your Parent tells his Child what to do. Learn to control your Parent and Child while listening. Let him express himself. Don't shoot out loaded questions that corner or trap him. Two games played from the Critical Parent ego state are CORNER, where the employee is trapped no matter what he says, and NIGYSOB. Another game sometimes used in combination with CORNER to trap the employee into a position in which he appears to be at fault is the YES, BUT game. Sometimes the game crops up in performance appraisals, especially when a supervisor's overly critical Parent harbors unrealistic performance expectations. However, the game can easily be played by the person being evaluated, as we shall see later on. In the following example, the boss is calling the shots.

> *Boss:* "On the whole, you've made some progress since the last rating period, but you've certainly got a long way to go."
>
> *Employee:* "I thought I was doing well. I met all the objectives we set."
>
> *Boss:* "Yes, but meeting objectives is a minimal achievement. That's expected."
>
> *Employee:* "Where is it you feel that I've fallen down?"
>
> *Boss:* "Well, for one thing I don't think you plan your time very well."
>
> *Employee:* "I never miss a deadline."
>
> *Boss:* "Yes, but you're missing the point. And here's another thing —you're not very cooperative."
>
> *Employee:* "I don't understand why you say that. I work well with others."
>
> *Boss:* "You may be *friendly* with others, but there have been times when you seemed reluctant to accept additional assignments."
>
> *Employee:* "Well, after all, I *was* busy."
>
> *Boss:* "Yes, but if you planned your work efficiently, you'd have more time—wouldn't you?"

Here, the employee is cut off from any avenue of retreat. Of course, it's easier to "fix" such a game so he can't win if you have neglected to set performance standards or develop a job description. To avoid playing such a game, learn to disregard Parent messages that may be telling you such things as, "Listen, friend, you shouldn't feel that way" or Child messages that prompt you to say, "If you knew the problems I have, you wouldn't bring me yours." Don't cross-examine or patronize: "Sure you're sore, but look how long it took *me* to make it in this company." This Child reaction is usually followed by a "right hook" from the Parent: "You know, you should be more patient . . . more thankful for the progress you've made here."

• Avoid admonishing the subordinate. Admonitions are Parent judgments that take such forms as "You've got the wrong attitude," "You've got to change your ways," "You don't know what's good for you," "If you had taken your education seriously, your career wouldn't be stalled at this point." These have the effect of intimidating the employee's Child and increasing the likelihood of childlike behavior—which may range from pouting to denial and rebellion.

• **Don't discount the employee's feelings and problems.** Instead of helping the employee, remarks like "You don't really have a problem" tend to hook his Child into action with counter-remarks or a withdrawal into angry silence. Discounting occurs whenever a person is made to feel that he is being put down, put off, ignored, underrated. The addition of sarcasm makes a particularly biting discount.

• **Don't supply the expected payoff in games.** It takes two or more people to play a game. If you have reason to believe that you are co-starring in some game, you can stop it cold by not offering the expected payoff. In the game of STUPID, for example, the obvious payoff is for you to put the employee down by implying or actually telling him that he's stupid. Simply refuse to do this. If you continue to use your Adult, chances are that the employee will feel incongruous in using his Child and will sooner or later start transacting from his Adult. Realizing that a deep need for recognition underlies much game-playing, you can set up conditions in which gold stamps are sought rather than the bad feelings that culminate from game-playing. An employee who repeatedly comes to work late or always turns in projects that are too little and too late is angling for a hard putdown in the form of a spoken or written admonition. You know that what he basically wants is recognition, attention. Try to swing him over into a cycle of positive strokes and productive actions. In any event, you should discuss his behavior with him before it reaches the disciplinary level. Remember to use your Adult and call upon his to map out a satisfactory plan for change.

• **Help the employee satisfy his Parent.** This is particularly necessary in order to help some hard-driving self-starters who seem unable to enjoy their successes or take a work break now and then. They find it difficult to relax because their Parent hounds them on to endless activity—even perfection. It may help to establish standards of sufficiency in work performance to keep them from "gilding the lily." Communicating expectations and giving timely recognition for achievement will help in most cases.

• **Give feedback.** From time to time, repeat in your words what the employee says; state the feelings that you think underlie his comments. This shows that you understand his or her feelings and that you consider them to be legitimate and acceptable. Such indications help comfort the employee's Child and activate his Adult. Specific feedback on performance during an appraisal can strengthen the employee's ability to test reality and feel competent in coping with his environment. It helps because it gives him objective measures of his performance against established standards. Generalities don't help an employee grow. What is needed is an action plan for change and development. Simply saying, "You're doing OK in all respects," may even make the employee feel discounted because he feels that you don't care enough to be specific. Honest, specific information on performance can give an employee a sense of increased OKayness if it is provided tactfully. Straight, honest evaluations are positive strokes in themselves—because they reflect close attention to the employee's growth.

• Stroke for being as well as for doing. Everyone likes to know that he is valued and accepted for himself, not exclusively for what he accomplishes at work. In giving positive strokes for the person, you recognize that there is a great deal more to him than is evident in task-related transactions and activities. The daily rituals of greeting and the pastimes people engage in during informal periods and breaks provide opportunities for this. A sincere expression of interest in how the employee is doing in his schoolwork, family activities, hobbies, or other interests will give strokes that value the person for being a special individual.

• Keep your transactions straight. Say what you mean and mean what you say. Avoid innuendo and ulterior transactions. If you say "That's a promising idea, John" or "Your chances of promotion are good" without meaning it, you are discounting the employee by giving crooked (deceptive) strokes.

• When reprimanding, separate the person from the act. When it's necessary to take disciplinary action, address yourself to the behavior involved, not to the personality or presumed attitudes of the employee. Doing this helps you use your Adult to the exclusion of your Parent. In turn, it tends to disarm the employee's Child by making it easier for him to focus on the behavior in question rather than brood on the threat to his self-esteem.

• Check out the employee's stamp collection. Is he getting enough gold stamps from his work? From his working relationships? Does he seem to have a favorite color in his stamp collection? How long has he been collecting? Ask yourself what you can do and what he can do to reduce the red and blue stamps and increase the gold.

• Use your Child in empathizing with him or her. It is possible to use both your Adult and your Child to convey a sense of understanding an employee's thoughts and feelings from his or her perspective. This is a kind of "putting yourself in the other person's ego states." It doesn't guarantee instant empathy, but it's a better approach to understanding an employee's position than relying on Adult reasoning alone.

• Enlist his Adult in recognizing his unrealistic wishes and fantasies.

Properly designed questions can help you do this. Sometimes a question can shake a person from lethargy into Adult awareness and commitment. For example, "What are you doing at this time to further your education so that you can be considered for promotion?" Too often, people harbor dreams of advancement but fail to act to make those dreams materialize. Some rely heavily on fantasies; like Cinderella, they pass their time waiting for someone or something to rescue them from dead-end jobs, under-utilization, and prolonged discontent. Another question that has proved helpful: "What do you think you'll be doing with us three years from now?"

• Be an active listener. Being listened to is a highly rewarding experience. In giving our full, undivided attention, we not only provide strokes that encourage the employee to talk more freely and express himself more completely, we also make him feel that he is important, that what happens to him matters. Such listening is an important preliminary to a change in behavior because it allows the employee to ventilate his feelings and put his thoughts together in a more precise and reasonable way. It helps him gain the approval of his Parent, ("It was good that you told it like it is") and satisfy his Child ("Gee, he really cares about my feelings").

• Listen for messages from the employee's Child. Phrases such as "I can't," "I won't," "I should," "I try, but" signal expressions that probably originate in his Child. They can tell you a great deal about his self-image, his hopes and fears, his doubts and uncertainties. The frequency of such Child expressions signals his degree of difficulty in communicating from his Adult. Consider whether such a difficulty springs from your relationship with him or from the circumstances that led to the interview.

• Counter the evasive strategy of the employee's manipulative Child. It may deliberately misinterpret your comments to evade the real issue and get its own way. Where this is a problem, simply have the employee repeat back to you his understanding of what you have said until it's clear that he *does* understand.

• Don't let periods of silence threaten your Child. Silence is a device that helps draw the employee out. It also gives you an opportunity to put your thoughts and feelings in order. Some supervisors get distressed when conversation stops. Their Parent may begin to send out such messages as "This shouldn't be happening," "You haven't organized this thing!" "You're putting the poor guy on the spot." These messages may pressure the supervisor to start speaking—but if he does, he's not likely to get to the heart of the employee's feelings and thoughts. He may even maneuver himself into a communication pattern in which the employee simply answers *yes* or *no* to questions without elaborating.

• Hook the Child's need to be creative. You might consider assigning him a special report, membership on special task-force committees, or research on new operating procedures; all are capable of allowing him to express his creativity on the job.

• Maintain your Adult in setting goals even when the opposition is stiff. The following extract from a counseling interview shows a supervisor making effective use of his Adult in combating the machinations of a subordinate skilled at playing YES, BUT.

> *Boss:* "Sam, I'd like to talk to you about your work. Will you join me in my office?"
>
> *Sam:* "Oh, okay, I'll be right with you."
>
> *Boss:* "I'll come right to the point. Your work has been deteriorating recently. Your productivity has fallen off and you've failed to meet three deadlines."
>
> *Sam:* "My work is as good as ever."
>
> *Boss:* "I'm not talking about how well you do things. I'm referring to how *much* you do and how *quickly* you do them."
>
> *Sam:* "Well, ever since we had to start using the new set-up procedure, nobody has been doing as much as before."
>
> *Boss:* "Sam, everyone in the section was consulted for their opinions before we installed it—including you. Nobody expressed any objections. If you want to talk about the production of the others, take a look at this production chart first."
>
> *Sam:* "Well, okay—so *they're* doing fine, but this new set-up throws *me* off."
>
> *Boss:* "Sam, your production started dropping before we began the new procedure."
>
> *Sam:* "Well, believe me, the new set-up procedure didn't help. Anyway, as they say, you can't teach an old dog new tricks."
>
> *Boss:* "Didn't your team leader explain it all to you?"
>
> *Sam:* "Yes, he did—but I guess I just didn't get it."
>
> *Boss:* "He told me he spent several hours with you."
>
> *Sam:* "I suppose he did—maybe I'm just thick."
>
> *Boss:* "We'll give you whatever assistance you need to understand it. If necessary, I'll arrange to streamline the production procedure on your line. Now, what about the deadlines, Sam—that's another matter."